A Tribute to Woody Guthrie & Leadbelly

Student Text

by
Will Schmid

Credits

Photos:

Unit 1—*African and European Roots of American Music*: Courtesy of the Library of Congress Folklife Division, California WPA collection and Todd/Sonkin collection; Library of Congress Photographic Archives, John and Alan Lomax collection and general collection.

Unit 2—*Woody Guthrie*: *Woody Guthrie* courtesy of the Smithsonian Institution Office of Folklife Programs; other photographs courtesy of the Library of Congress Folklife Division, California WPA collection.

Unit 3—*Leadbelly*: *Huddie Ledbetter* courtesy of the Smithsonian Institution Office of Folklife Programs; Reed Camp, South Carolina inmates courtesy of Library of Congress Photographic Archives, John and Alan Lomax collection.

Unit 4—*The New Generation*: *Bob Dylan* © 1989 Ken Regan/Camera 5; *Arlo Guthrie* courtesy of Harold Leventhal Mgt., Inc.; *Emmylou Harris* by Caroline Greyshock 0688; *Little Richard* by John E. Reed; *Taj Mahal* by Susan Wilson; *John Cougar Mellencamp* © 1989 PolyGram; *Willie Nelson* by Beth Gwinn; *Pete Seeger* by Curt Koehler; *Bruce Springsteen* by Todd Kaplan; *Sweet Honey In The Rock* by Roland L. Freeman; *Doc Watson* by Peter Figen; *Brian Wilson* courtesy of Sire Records.

Page design, typesetting, engraving and editing by Will Schmid in cooperation with MENC staff.

Copyright © 1991
Music Educators National Conference
1902 Association Drive, Reston, Virginia 22091
All rights reserved.
Printed in the United States of America
ISBN 0-940796-84-8

Table of Contents

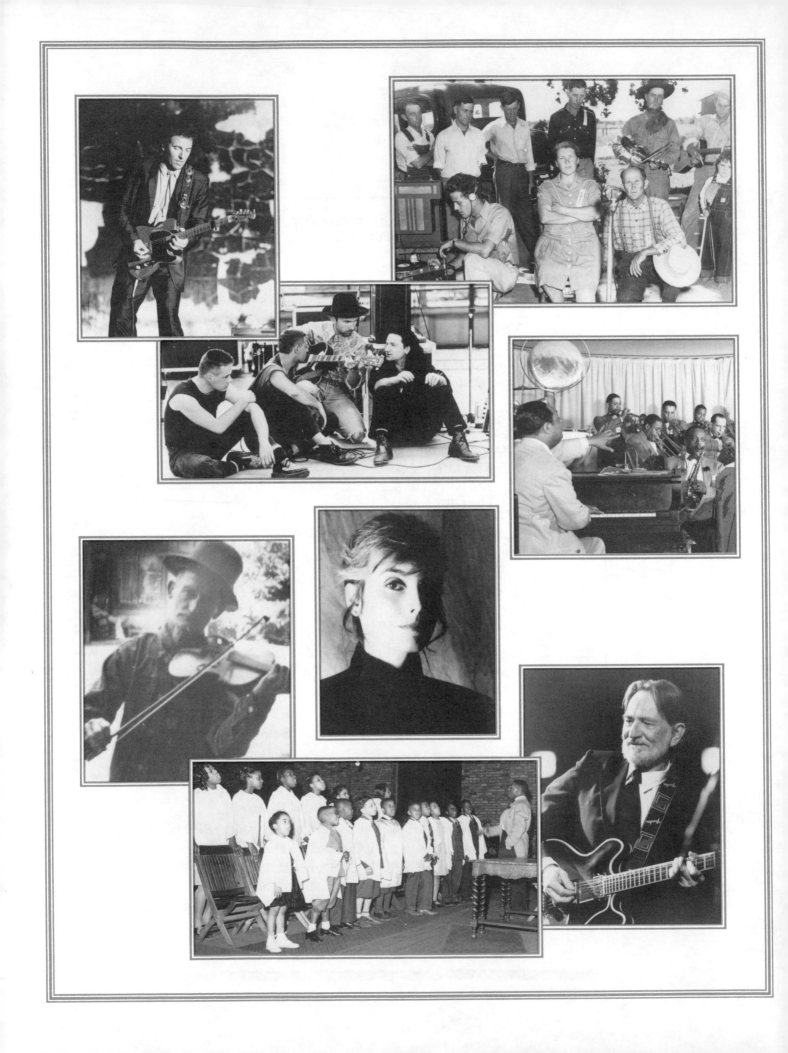

African and European Roots of American Music

After reading UNIT ONE and doing the activities you will be able to:

- Describe how songs become folk songs through oral tradition and variation.

- List contributions to American music made by Africans and Europeans.

- Identify elements of African and European musical style in popular recordings.

- Describe how "chart hits" sometimes turn into folk music.

- Identify types of music created by African- and European-Americans over the last 200 years.

- Write your own parodies—new words to old tunes.

VOCABULARY

Autoharp	Hillbilly
Ballad	Jazz
Banjo	Lyrics
Blues	Oral tradition
Broadside	Parody
Call and response	Popular song
Country & western	Race records
Cover recording	Ragtime
Fiddle	Rhythm & blues
Folk song	Spiritual
Gospel	Syncopation
Guitar	Work song
Gutbucket	Variation
Harmony	Zither

In UNIT ONE you will learn how Africans and Europeans brought their music to America and how these root traditions combined and grew into many different musical styles. Long before African- and European-Americans learned to live together with any sense of equality, they were attracted by each other's music and to the music of other cultural groups. Who knows how large a contribution music has made in creating a world where people live in mutual respect?

People make new songs in a variety of ways—some write them down and some work orally (or aurally, by ear). Once created, songs take on a life of their own. Some change to suit the times or the singer, some stubbornly remain the same, and some simply disappear. In listening to the *A Vision Shared* recording or video tape, you will hear how popular singers have brought music born of an oral tradition into the modern world of recorded music. In this unit you will learn how these forces work and how songs have changed to reflect America's history.

> *I usually figure a song that I compose is like a child; mine to control only as long as it sticks around the house. When it goes out into the world, it grows and has a life of its own, or maybe dies . . . in the long run, it is those who listen to the song throughout the world who will decide which version will last, and which will be forgotten.*
>
> —*Pete Seeger*

Oral Tradition and Folk Music

Once music is created, it is usually shared with other people. In sharing a song or instrumental piece, the music often changes. Music changes more when it is not written down and is passed from person to person by word of mouth—a process called **oral tradition**. In this section you will see how oral tradition has affected American music and created a type of music called **folk music**.

When Words Change

Sometimes musical **lyrics** (words) change because they are misunderstood. Have you ever taken a phone message and written down a stranger's name with a highly original spelling? Perhaps you heard a rock song and thought the singer was singing one thing, only to find out later that it was something else. For example, there is the classic story of the person who thought "The Star Spangled Banner" began "José, can you see?"

Composers sometimes put new words to an old tune. The result is often called a **parody** or **take-off**. Think of the many songs you know that have several different sets of words. Here are a few examples to start your list:

"On Top of Old Smokey" → "On Top of Spaghetti"
"When Johnny Comes Marching Home" → "Ants Go Marching"
"Greensleeves" → "What Child Is This"

People make up new words to suit the needs of the moment, whether poking fun at a political candidate, writing a religious song, protesting an environmental problem, or just having a good time. When the printing press was invented around 1450, people started printing new words to songs called **broadsides** and selling them in the streets. Today, if you go to a meeting and receive a sheet with new words to an old song you are getting a modern-day broadside.

Ballads (story songs) came from Europe and exist in many different **variations** with different sets of verses. You know what happens when a rumor starts going around school—it often results in wild stories that have little to do with truth. The oral tradition works in this same way with ballad lyrics. In the process of making a ballad his or her own, a singer might personalize it by changing the location or the names of the main characters. Sometimes singers forget the original words and are forced to make up some new ones on the spot while they are singing. When this happens, they sometimes borrow words from other songs with a similar story line. Below are examples of similar lines that appear in various English ballads when someone is about to die.

O mother, O mother, go dig my grave,
Go dig it wide and deep;

O father, O father go dig my grave,
Go dig it deep and narrow;

O mother, O mother, go make my bed,
And fix it wide and smooth;

Go dig my grave both wide and deep,
A marble stone at my head and feet;

In the African-American tradition, words are often improvised as part of a **call and response** form where the leader makes up a line and the rest of the group answers with a repeated response. This form was used in both **work songs** and **spirituals**. A typical example comes from the song "Wade in the Water," which uses a common two-line rhyming structure.

Look at those children dressed in white,
Wade in the water,
Must be the children of the Israelite.
Wade in the water.

Look at those children dressed in red,
Wade in the water,
Must be the children that Moses led.
Wade in the water.

See examples of these two-line rhythming verses in Leadbelly's "Rock Island Line" (page 42). This same two-line structure carries over into the **blues**, but the first line is repeated to make an AAB rhyme scheme.

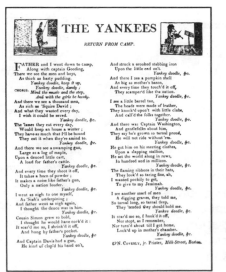

18th century Revolutionary War broadside

Both Woody Guthrie and Leadbelly borrowed old tunes to make new songs. Both "Ramblin' 'Round" and "Roll On, Columbia" (page 47) are new words written to the tune of "Goodnight Irene" (page 36).

When Music Changes

A twenty-verse song can become rather boring if the melody is sung exactly the same each time. Good singers see to it that this does not happen by working subtle variations into the melody of some verses. You can make melody variations by changing the rhythm, changing some of the pitches in the melody, or by adding ornamentation. Listen to the different versions of "This Land Is Your Land" as good examples of melody variation and individual singing on the *A Vision Shared* video tape or recording.

Ballads sometimes retain the basic story but have many different melodies. Here are the beginnings of three different variations of the broadside ballad "Froggie Went A-Courtin'." Notice how different the melodies are:

Example 1

The frog went court - in' and he did ride, a - huh,

Example 2

Frog went a - court - in' and he did ride,

Example 3

The frog went court - in' and he did ride,

The African-American call and response form gives the song leader an opportunity to improvise new melodies. This adds variety to the music and gives energy to the group singing the response. You can hear this improvisation in worksongs, spirituals, gospel, blues, and jazz. Listen to Sweet Honey in The Rock sing Leadbelly's call and response song, "Gray Goose," on the *A Vision Shared* recording.

From Sheet Music to Folk Song

A **popular song** written by a composer usually becomes a piece of sheet music. If the song is sung by enough people, it becomes part of oral tradition and results in the kinds of variations you have just studied. When a song is part of oral tradition for a long enough period of time, people call it a **folk song**.

In 1838 the number-one popular song of the year was "Rosin the Beau." Below is the original sheet music cover and some of the parodies that followed during the 19th century.

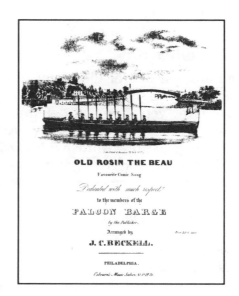

OLD ROSIN THE BEAU

Favourite Comic Song

Dedicated with much respect

to the members of the

FALCON BARGE

by the Publisher.

Arranged by

J. C. BECKELL.

PHILADELPHIA.

1838 – original words	I live for the good of my nation, And my sons are all growing low; But I hope that the next generation Will resemble old Rosin the Beau.
1840 – the first U.S. Presidential campaign where songs and slogans played a big part.	You can't make a song to Van Buren, Because his long name will not do; There's nothin' about him allurin', As there is about Tippecanoe!
1860 – a version that helped to elect Abraham Lincoln President.	Hurrah for the choice of the nation! Our chieftain so brave and so true; We'll go for the great Reformation— For Lincoln and Liberty too!
late 19th century – "Acres of Clams" – how a man moved west and settled in Puget Sound.	I've traveled all over this country, Prospecting and digging for gold. I've tunneled, hydraulicked and cradled, And, I have been frequently sold.

The process of turning popular sheet music into parodies continues into the 1990's as popular songs are reworked to become radio and television commercials. Find some examples.

African and European Singing Styles in America

The way people sing reflects the way they live. For example—people who live and work together on an equal basis tend to sing easily in a group with no leader. In contrast—people who live and work more individually need a strong leader to pull them together at work or when singing. In this section you will study contrasts in African- and European-American singing styles.

What to Listen for

Words are just one of the many important elements of a song style. Whether a song has many words or very few will determine how that song will be sung. **Many African-American songs use few words with much repetition.** This makes for great group singing. It makes songs easier to remember, and repetition gives power to the message by driving it home. In contrast, **many European-American songs are very wordy with little repetition.** In these traditions, solo singing is more common, words must often be written down to remember them, many words can spell out subtle shades of meaning, and consonants must be carefully enunciated or the words will not be understood.

Can you identify which verses below come from the African- American tradition and which come from the European-American tradition?

1. Oh____ it may be,____
   Oh____ it may be,____
   Oh____ it may be,____
   It may be the last time, I don't know.____

2. Go bring me a bag of your father's gold,
   Likewise your mother's fee,
   And the two best horses out of the stall,
   Where there stand thirty and three.

3. Oh, what can you do in a case like that?
   Oh, what can you do but stamp on your hat
   Or on your brother, on your toothbrush,
   Or anything that's helpless?

4. Sun gonna shine on my back door some day,
   Sun gonna shine on my back door some day,
   Wind gonna rise up and blow my blues away.

Below is a "Style Chart" that shows the basic characteristics of the African- and European-American singing styles. Apply the Style Chart to both old and new song recordings, and determine whether the singing style is basically African-American, European-American, or a mixture of both. Remember that the Style Chart only shows basic tendencies—you will always be able to find exceptions.

THE STYLE CHART

African-American	European-American
few words -------------	many words
relaxed consonants----	articulated consonants
group singing -----------	solo singing
buzzy or raspy tone--------	clear tone
open-throated tone-----	somewhat nasal tone
syncopated rhythms-------	on-beat rhythms
3-against-2 meters--------	one meter
obvious beat -------	subtle or hidden beat
bending melody notes------	straight melodies
much melody sliding ----	some melody sliding
added words/syllables-------	regular words

The characteristics given in the Style Chart show the styles of singing derived from African cultures south of the Sahara Desert and European cultures found in northern Europe. Other styles of singing exist in both Africa and Europe—for example, the Moslem styles of northern Africa or the eastern European styles found in Slavic countries.

Many Africans south of the Sahara prefer a "buzzy" tone on their musical instruments and in their voices. They often attach bottle caps or loose pieces of metal to instruments to make a continuous buzzing sound.

8

African-American Contributions to American Music

Musical Instruments

Percussion instruments including **drums** of all sizes, **rattles, xylophones, marimbas,** and **bells** are widely used in Africa south of the Sahara. Before the Civil War, slaves in the United States were not permitted to use drums for fear that they could be used to signal an uprising. Regardless of this ban on drums, rhythm continued to be an important element in many forms of African-American music. In today's music, the important place of the drum set in jazz, rock, and Latin-American styles is directly due to African influence.

Stringed instruments also are widely played in Africa as accompaniment to singing or in combination with other instruments. The **banjo,** developed in America, was based on an African prototype that had a stick neck stuck through a gourd, turtle shell, or other hollow resonator covered with a stretched animal skin. The **gutbucket** or washtub bass probably developed from another plucked African instrument called the mosquito drum (a flexible young tree bent over and tied to an animal skin stretched over a hole in the ground). The preference for the plucked, slapped or popped (as opposed to bowed) bass in styles like jazz, rock or Latin-American music shows the African influence on a European stringed instrument.

Musical Styles

African-American **work songs** sung during the 19th century included hollers, axe and hammer songs, railroad track-lining songs, and a wide variety of rhythmic songs sung to make the work seem easier. Sweet Honey in the Rock's version of Leadbelly's "Bring Me L'il' Water, Silvy" is an interesting musical arrangement. Compare it to Leadbelly's original on the *Folkways: The Original Vision* recording. "Take This Hammer" (page 43) is a rock-busting hammer song from the experience of black prisoners during the 1930's Great Depression. Notice the "wah" in the lyrics to indicate the hammer blow.

Spirituals—great songs of faith born out of slavery—represent one of America's important song treasures. Some of the hallmarks of the African-American spiritual style in addition to those from the Style Chart are:

- call and response form
- 2-line interchangeable rhyming lines
- Judgement Day theme
- Old Testament Biblical themes

After the Civil War, African-American colleges such as Fisk University sent their choirs to tour the northern United States and Europe. Groups such as the Fisk Jubilee Singers helped to popularize many of the spirituals that are still widely known today.

In the 1920's a new style of black religious song called **gospel** added a new dimension to the spiritual tradition. The acknowledged leader of the gospel movement was Thomas Dorsey. This new style added instruments such as the piano and (at a later time) the Hammond electric organ. It also featured solo quartets or other special performers. Many of the greatest African-American singers of this century, such as Mahalia Jackson or Aretha Franklin, got their start singing in the local church gospel choir.

In contrast to the group singing of work songs and spirituals, **blues** were solo songs that gave vent to the frustrations and personal troubles of the African-American. Early blues from the Mississippi Delta or Texas—called **country blues**—were sung with guitar accompaniment. These early singers often sang three phrases (AAB) that used twelve measures of music—a form called **12-bar blues.** Leadbelly's song "The Bourgeois Blues" (page 31) is an example of this form. The second stage of the blues style was the 1920's **classic blues** featuring female singers such as Bessie Smith with a small jazz band accompaniment using players such as the great trumpet player Louis Armstrong. When players such as Muddy Waters used electric guitars and instruments such as saxophones during the 1940's and 50's, the style became known as **urban blues** or **rhythm and blues.** Eventually the rhythm and blues style gave birth in 1955 to rock 'n' roll, which featured many songs in the 12-bar blues form. Rock 'n' roll stars such as Elvis, Chuck Berry, or Little Richard, who appears on the *A Vision Shared* video tape, sang many early hit songs in this style during the period from 1955 to 1959.

Around the turn of the century, piano styles such as **ragtime** and early forms of **jazz** developed within African-American communities. These fresh new styles, with their exciting syncopated rhythms, quickly became popular with mixed audiences throughout America and even Europe. In the 1920's when phonograph records became practical and less expensive, many of the early jazz bands and blues performers recorded their music on African-American labels such as Paramount or Okeh. Recordings by African-American performers were known up through the 1940's as **race records**. When a race record became a big hit, a **cover** recording was usually made by a white performer to take advantage of its popularity. The practice of making cover recordings can be seen up through 1950's rock 'n' roll with Elvis' version of Joe Turner's "Shake, Rattle and Roll."

In the 1960's the word **soul** began to replace the term **rhythm and blues** as a name for recordings made by African-Americans. By the 60's many elements of African-American music had been absorbed by white performers.

European-American Contributions to American Music

Musical Instruments

Europeans brought musical instruments such as **fiddles** (violins), **concertinas, guitars, mandolins, zithers,** and **pianos** with them to America. During the 18th and 19th centuries, the fiddle was probably the most portable and practical instrument used in the westward expansion of America. A fiddler who could play a lively dance tune was a welcome member of most communities. The piano became a parlor fixture during the 19th century, and a healthy sheet-music industry sprang up to meet the demand for songs by such composers as Stephen Foster. American guitar companies such as C.F. Martin were established as early as 1840, and the guitar gradually grew to a popularity that matched the piano in its impact on American folk and popular music. In the late 1800's a new American instrument called the **Autoharp** was created from a German zither, and it quickly

became a popular folk instrument that is still used in school music programs. Wind instruments such as the cornet, trumpet, saxophone, clarinet, trombone, and others were quickly incorporated into jazz and other forms of American popular music.

Musical Styles

The **ballad** or story song is one of the most important musical contributions made by European-Americans. Ballads from England, Scotland, Ireland, or France became prototypes for sea, railroad, cowboy, lumberjack, and farmer songs sung from Maine to California. Immigrants moving westward during the 19th century often made up their own versions or parodies of well-known ballads such as "Rosin the Beau," which was discussed on page 7.

A form of white **spiritual** known today as the Sacred Harp spiritual or shape-note hymn came into being during the same period (1800-1860) that gave rise to the African-American spiritual. The different-shaped notes were used as a method of learning how to read music. Perhaps the best known song in this style is "Amazing Grace," written by a repentant slave trader who dedicated the rest of his life to fighting the evils of slavery. In the 1920's **gospel** music was created which often featured quartets or family bands who accompanied themselves on guitars, Autoharps, fiddles, or **string band** instruments.

Fiddle tunes such as reels and jigs were a staple of life in 19th century America. Tunes such as "Turkey in the Straw" or "Arkansas Traveler" were played for dances and eventually used in stage productions such as the minstrel show. Today these same fiddle tunes are still part of a branch of country music called **bluegrass**, which features fiddle, guitar, mandolin, and the five-string banjo—an instrument that crossed over from African-American music.

In the 1920's when phonograph records became practical and radios found a place in most American homes, a new style of European-American music was born. Record promoters went into Appalachia and the Southwest to find new recording talent. The new style was dubbed **hillbilly**, and the name stuck for about twenty-five years. The southeastern Appalachian style followed the lead of the Carter

Family, and family bands sprang up often featuring duets by brothers or sisters. The southwestern region followed the lead of Jimmie Rodgers and developed a Texas cowboy style as sung by the famous movie cowboys Gene Autry and Roy Rogers. As the 1930's turned to the '40's, the name hillbilly gradually gave way to the term **country and western** (which showed the original southeastern and southwestern roots). Performers from both styles were featured on radio shows such as Nashville's *Grand Ole Opry* and Chicago's *National Barn Dance*. After World War II, the country and western style gradually incorporated electric instruments, a drum set, and in the late '60's—some elements of the rock style. Eventually the term **country** was used to describe this new style of music.

Elvis Presley, star of '50's rock 'n' roll, showed an interesting combination of style influences. In addition to the African-American rhythm and blues discussed earlier, he was also much influenced by European-American hillbilly and gospel styles. Before he became a rock 'n' roll star, he had sung the country and western song "Old Shep" on Nashville's Grand Ole Opry.

Perhaps the most important musical element that came from Europe is **harmony**—the functional use of chords—sometimes called the "vertical" element in music. Listen to church hymns or chords on a guitar to hear good examples of harmony at work.

In the 20th century, American popular music absorbed both African- and European-American styles in a variety of different mixtures. On the stage, the minstrel show gave way to vaudeville, revues, and finally the Broadway musical. Ragtime and blues were incorporated into jazz in its many forms—dixieland, boogie woogie, swing, bebop, and many more. Rhythm and blues (R&B) and country and western (C&W) combined to form rock 'n' roll and the many varieties of rock with prefixes like hard (rock), psychedelic, punk, country, and heavy metal. Almost all American popular music today is a fusion of elements from African and European musical influences. It will be interesting to see how American music absorbs styles from other parts of the world in the global village of the 1990's.

Unit Review

REVIEW QUESTIONS

1. What is the oral tradition, and how does music change as a result of it?

2. How can popular sheet music turn into folk music? Can you give examples of songs where this has happened?

3. How many of the singing style characteristics can you remember from the Style Chart on page 8? Divide a blank page into two columns headed by African-American and European-American; then list as many style characteristics as you can remember. Check your work.

4. What contributions have African-Americans made to American popular music? Instruments? Types of music?

5. What contributions have European-Americans made to American popular music? Instruments? Types of music?

VOCABULARY DISCUSSION

1. Discuss how **race records** were often **covered** by white performers.

2. How do popular singers and instrumentalists use the **variation** idea to make their music more interesting? Find recordings to illustrate your points.

3. What are two different meanings for the label **rhythm and blues**?

4. How was the **country & western** style a mixture of several regional types of music?

5. Do we still have **work songs** today?

CREATIVE PROJECTS

• Write new words to a well-known tune.

• Apply the Style Chart (page 8) to some of your favorite songs.

• Make a gutbucket and form a jug band with washboard, guitars, and kazoos.

• Select one of the songs in the back of the book and see if you can perform it in different styles such as C&W or R&B.

Woody Guthrie

He really believed in the power of music to make people alive.
—*Millard Lampell, Almanac Singers*

LEARNING OBJECTIVES

After reading UNIT TWO and doing the activities you will be able to:

- Describe the Dust Bowl and Great Depression of the 1930s and tell how Woody Guthrie was both a product and a shaper of those times.
- List contributions Woody Guthrie made to American music.
- Identify other musicians associated with and influenced by him.
- Describe Guthrie's musical style, his roots in hillbilly music, and his influence on the Folk Revival of the 1950s and '60s folk-rock .

WOODY'S SONGS

In UNIT TWO you will learn about the life and music of Woody Guthrie, an American original. The video tape *A Vision Shared* testifies to the power of his influence on generations of singers and songwriters. He became the model for guitar-playing folksingers who sing their original songs rooted in the folk tradition—songs about social justice, the environment, the down and out, the right to a decent job with honest pay, or the American dream.

What you will also find here is the portrait of a man whose life speaks to the major issues for our day. Woody was a citizen of the world who went far beyond the nationalistic values of his time. He was also completely at home with people of all races and colors. So take this opportunity to learn from his music and his life.

> *Woody is just Woody. Thousands of people do not know he had any other name. He is just a voice and a guitar. He sings the songs of a people and I suspect that he is, in a way, that people. Harsh voiced and nasal, his guitar hanging like a tire iron on a rusty rim, there is nothing sweet about Woody, and there is nothing sweet about the songs he sings. But there is something more important for those who will listen. There is the will of a people to endure and fight against oppression. I think we call this the American spirit.*
>
> —*John Steinbeck*

Woody's Life

The Early Days

Woodrow Wilson Guthrie was born July 14, 1912 in Okemah, Oklahoma. Woody had this to say about his home town:

> Okemah, Oklahoma, where I come from was one of the singingest, square-dancingest, drinkingest, preachingest, walkingest, talkingest, laughingest, cryingest, shootingest, fist-fightingest, bleedingest, gamblingest, gun, club and razor carryingest of our ranch and farm towns, because it blossomed into one of our first Oil Boom Towns.

By age 14, his mother was institutionalized with what was later diagnosed as Huntington's chorea, his father was crippled and out of money, and his sister Clara was killed in a fire. Woody and his older brother Roy were left to watch after themselves. So he left town and travelled to Houston, Texas and the Gulf . . .

> doing all kind of odd jobs, hoeing figs, orchards, pickin' grapes, hauling wood, helping carpenters and cement men, working with water well drillers. I carried my harmonica and played in barber shops, at [shoe] shine stands, in front of shows, around the pool halls, . . . sang and played with Negroes, Indians, whites, farmers, town folks, truck drivers, and with every kind of singers you can think of. I learned all the tricks of strings and music and all of the songs that I could remember and learn by ear.

He returned to the Texas panhandle town of Pampa for a few years where he played in a hillbilly band, worked at odd jobs, married Mary Jennings and had two children. Woody also worked as a local musician along with his dad's half-brother Jeff.

> Jeff . . . taught me how to chord on the guitar. After a while I was rattling around with him playing my way at the ranch and farm house dances. We worked our way up to playing inside of the city limits, and then for the banquet thrown by the Chamber of Commerce. We played for rodeos, centennials, carnivals, parades, fairs, just bustdown parties, and played several nights and days a week just to hear our own boards rattle and our strings roar around in the wind. It was along in these days I commenced singing, I guess it was singing.

The Dust Bowl

In 1929 the New York Stock Market crashed signaling the beginning of a Great Depression that would last well into the 1940s and World War II. During the 1930s, great dust storms followed on the heels of drought and blew away the topsoil on many of the Great Plains states such as Oklahoma. Farmers lost their homes and land, banks went bankrupt (there was no FDIC then), and many people were out of work.

Woody, like many others, took to the road in search of food, shelter, and a job to support his family. He headed for California and found work as a sign painter and musician.

> I hit the highway to look around for a place for us to go. I carried my pockets full of paint brushes and my guitar slung across my back. I painted all kinds of window signs, posters, show cards, banners, car and truck signs, in the daylight and played with my hat down on the old saloon floor after night had set in. Got to California and went up and down the west coast a few times, found a cousin of mine, Jack, and we took a fifteen minute radio program in order to collect us enough prestige around at the saloons to ask for a two dollar guarantee for six hours.

His songs **"I Ain't Got No Home"** (p. 39), **"Going Down the Road"** (p. 35), **"Do Re Mi"** (p. 34), **"Deportee"** (p. 33), and **"Vigilante Man"** (p. 46) describe in music what the novelist John Steinbeck wrote about in *Grapes of Wrath* or Dorothea Lange treated in her photographs. He got a job singing his songs on radio station KFVD and wrote a regular newspaper column for the *People's Daily World*.

I saw the hundreds of thousands of stranded, broke, hungry, idle, miserable people that lined the highways all out through the leaves and the underbrush. I heard these people sing in their jungle [hobo] camps and in their Federal Work Camps and sang songs I made up for them over the air waves.

When Woody's radio job produced enough income, his younger brother George joined him in California. Shortly thereafter, he bought a house and sent for Mary and the two girls. Later, they had a son, Bill Rogers Guthrie, named after the famous humorist Will Rogers and an actor friend Will Geer.

Throughout his life Woody often got the wanderlust. The songs **"Hard Travelin'"** (p. 37), **"Ramblin' 'Round"** (p. 47) and **"Hobo's Lullaby"** (p. 38) tell about his travels during the 1930s. He took the family back to Oklahoma, borrowed $35 from his brother Roy and headed off to New York City where he stayed with actor Will Geer and his wife. During this period he met **Alan Lomax**, who with his father John had recorded American folk songs for the Library of Congress. In March of 1940, Lomax invited Guthrie down to Washington D.C. where he interviewed him and recorded his songs. It was during this same period that Woody met **Pete Seeger**, whom he described as "a long tall string bean kid from up in New England." Together with Alan Lomax they collaborated on a landmark book entitled *Hard Hitting Songs for Hard-Hit People* (published over twenty-five years later), which along with the twelve *Dust Bowl Ballads* recorded for Victor serve as a first-rate documentary history of the period.

Guthrie's strong support of organized labor took him and Pete Seeger on the road singing songs for the movement. **"Union Maid"** (p. 45) was composed during this trip. Guthrie became a mentor for Pete Seeger, who returned the favor years later by teaching Guthrie's songs to several new generations of singers. During this trip, Guthrie and Seeger stopped off in Tennessee at the Highlander Center, a leadership training camp for the Labor Movement and later the Civil Rights Movement.

When Woody got back to New York City he became increasingly popular and successful as a radio singer on shows such as the *Pursuit of Happiness* and *Cavalcade of America* (In the 1940s, music on the radio was live, not recorded.). While this success brought in more money than he had ever made, it forced him to sing songs and commercials that he didn't like.

I got disgusted with the whole sissified and nervous rules of censorship on all of my songs and ballads, and drove off down the road across the southern states again.

World War II and Beyond

Roosevelt's New Deal had put people back to work rebuilding America. Like Guthrie, artists such as **Thomas Hart Benton** (painting), **Martha Graham** (dance), or **John Steinbeck** (literature) were recording the American experience. While in California, Guthrie was contracted to write songs for the Bonneville Power Administration to promote the Grand Coulee and Bonneville dams. The song **"Roll On, Columbia"** (p. 47) was written for this purpose.

When Woody returned to New York City, he joined Pete Seeger and the **Almanac Singers** who gave Sunday afternoon concerts called **"hootenannies"** in the basement of their Greenwich Village house and other places. When America entered World War II after Pearl Harbor, Woody joined the Merchant Marine and shipped out with **Cisco Houston**, a singer/guitarist with whom he would eventually make a series of records for Moe Asch and Folkways Records. Other musical associates included the **Weavers, Josh White, Leadbelly** and **Sonny Terry**. Woody's best known song **"This Land Is Your Land"** (p. 44) was written during this period as a response to a World War II favorite "God Bless America."

Woody was divorced and remarried twice, and had other children including **Arlo** who appears on the *A Vision Shared* video tape. Woody spent the last eleven years of his life in hospitals suffering from Huntington's chorea and died on October 3, 1967 in New York City.

Woody's Music

Woody Guthrie's musical life is a testament to the notion that making music is as natural as breathing or eating. He drew his inspiration and power from the people.

The worst thing that can happen to you is to cut yourself loose from the people. And the best thing is to sort of vaccinate yourself right into the big streams and blood of the people.

> *I CANNOT HELP BUT LEARN MY MOST*
> *FROM YOU WHO COUNT YOURSELF LEAST*
> *AND CANNOT HELP BUT FEEL MY BEST WHEN*
> *YOU THAT NEED ME MOST ASK ME TO HELP*
> *YOU AND I NEVER DID KNOW*
> *EXACTLY WHY THIS WAS*
> *THAT IS JUST THE WAY WE ARE BUILT*
>
> —*Woody Guthrie*

He loved to sing and he believed in the power of music to help make things better.

Oh I love to hear houses sing, I love to hear windows yell. I remember livin' in the hope that when I got out of those old pesky Army camps, I'd hear every door and every window, just for one night, sing all night long,'til a new day cracked. I ask ya Mr. President, please, let everybody everywhere, for just one night, sing all night long: Love songs, work songs, new hope songs. That would cure every soul in our jails and asylums, and most of the sick in our hospitals.

He believed that music was for everybody, not just a select group, and he believed that anyone could make his or her own songs.

You know you are as good a songwriter as there is, but you might not believe it. If you don't believe it, that's why you're not. All you have to do is sit down and write up what's wrong and how to fix it. That's all there is to it.

He lived a life that recognized the values of men and women of all races, colors and creeds. The following quote comes out of the series of recordings he made for Folkways Records with Cisco Houston and Sonny Terry (harmonica).

I talked to Sonny about these things in his art and he tells me that he is blind and that he still knows that his people can see a world where we all vote, eat, work, talk, plan and think together and with all of our spokes and wheels rolling and all of our selves well dressed and well housed and well fed. These are the things that the artist in Blind Sonny Terry knows and sees in his blindness. These are the upland echoes of the things that stir and sing along his big muddies. These are the plans and visions seen in the kiss and whisper of tall tree jack pines falling into the chutes to make your papery pulps. These are the freedoms. These are the samples of the kinds of soul art that the Negro, Indian, Mexican, the Irish, the Jew, the Russian, the Greek, Italian, all of us, have to bring to be seen and heard.

Woody's music reflected the hillbilly singing and instrumental style. He was extremely prolific and wrote almost every day. Mill Lampell said this in *A Tribute to Woody Guthrie:*

Woody's guitar playing wasn't much. Sort of casual, down-home, Carter Family style with some Jimmie Rodgers licks thrown in. He blew some free-wheeling mouth harp. Played pretty fair mandolin. And a wild fiddle, holding it tucked under his ribs the country way. In a pinch, he could also get some clackety music out of a couple of soup spoons.

Woody performed about the same way he drove. As though his brakes were shot and he wasn't too sure what was coming next. His playing was peppered with sharps, flats, hit and misses, and several notes never before heard on land, sea or air. But it was harsh and honest, exploding with life.

Nobody knows just how many songs Woody made up. A collector claims to have counted over a thousand. But that would only be the ones Woody took the trouble to write down. It wouldn't include the songs that slipped away in the dusty wind, the ones that vanished in the clank and rattle of a fast freight crossing through the hills in the darkness.

Following are some of Woody's best known songs for which he used existing melodies.

"Union Maid" from "Redwing"

"Sinking of the Reuben James" from "Wildwood Flower"

"This Land Is Your Land" from "Little Darlin' Pal of Mine"

"Tom Joad" from "John Hardy"

"Jesus Christ" from "Jesse James"

"The Philadelphia Lawyer" from "The Jealous Lover"

"Pastures of Plenty" from "Pretty Polly"

"Roll On, Columbia" and "Ramblin' 'Round" from "Goodnight Irene"

Woody's Influence

Woody Guthrie set the mold for generations of singers and songwriters. Foremost among his musical associates was **Pete Seeger**, dean of the American folk movement since 1950. After touring and singing with Guthrie throughout the 1940s, Seeger formed a new group called the **Weavers** and the **Folk Revival** of the 1950s was born. The movie *Wasn't That A Time!* reviews this period when **coffee houses** were the place to hear folk music, poetry and social commentary, and singer/guitar players gathered in living rooms for **hootenannies** [group sings]. Other Folk Revival groups that followed the Weavers' success were the **Kingston Trio**, the **Brothers Four**, the **Limelighters**, the **Chad Mitchell Trio**, and **Peter, Paul, and Mary**. Solo folksingers included **Joan Baez**, **Tom Paxton**, **Odetta**, **Judy Collins**, and **Ramblin' Jack Elliott**. All of these artists recorded Woody's songs.

In 1960, a young fellow by the name of Robert Zimmerman attended the University of Minnesota, changed his name to **Bob Dylan**, and dedicated his life to becoming the next Woody Guthrie. Dylan read and quoted Guthrie from his autobiography *Bound for Glory* or from *Sing Out!* Magazine, dressed like Guthrie, listened to all his records, sang, and played guitar and harmonica in the Guthrie style. Bob Dylan made a pilgrimage to New York City to visit Woody in the hospital and was so elated after seeing him that he exclaimed . . .

> I know Woody . . . I know him and met him and saw him and sang to him. I know Woody!

Dylan met Seeger and others in the New York folk community and was soon a rising star in the Greenwich Village coffeehouses. Dylan's "Song to Woody" is an homage to his mentor set to the tune of Guthrie's "1913 Massacre."

In 1965, Dylan and others such as the **Byrds** created an interesting blend of **folk-rock**. Others who recorded Guthrie songs at this time included **Country Joe and the Fish**, **Jesse Colin Young** and **Ry Cooder**. At the time of Woody Guthrie's death in 1967, the nation's young had heeded his clarion call for change and were challenging the establishment at every turn.

Unit Review

1. How do the songs "I Ain't Got No Home," "Going Down the Road," "Do Re Mi," "Deportee" and "Vigilante Man" reflect Guthrie's dust bowl and California experiences?

2. Who were the early influences on Woody's musical style? What instruments did he play?

3. How does the song, "This Land Is Your Land" compare to other patriotic American songs such as "God Bless America" or "America the Beautiful"?

4. Who were some of the musicians influenced by Woody Guthrie?

5. During the 1950s McCarthy era, Guthrie was accused of being "un-American." Why do you think he was so controversial? What would Woody sing about if he were alive today?

MORE ABOUT WOODY GUTHRIE

If you would like to read more about Woody and hear more of his music, try these:

Guthrie, Woody. *Bound for Glory*. New York: Dutton, 1943. —his autobiography

Hard Travelin': Woody Guthrie. (MGM/UA release 600884). —70-min. video

Klein, Joe. *Woody Guthrie: A Life*. New York: Knopf, 1980.

Lomax, Alan, Woody Guthrie and Pete Seeger. *Hard Hitting Songs for Hard-Hit People*. New York: Music Sales, 1967.

The Woody Guthrie Songbook. New York: Woody Guthrie Publications, 1976.

Recordings —see listing of other Guthrie recordings on liner notes to *Folkways: The Original Vision*. Smithsonian Folkways.

CREATIVE PROJECTS

• Try to find a way to see Jeff Waxman's play, *Woody Guthrie's American Song*, and/or make your own musical play about Woody (idea— What if Woody were to come back for a visit?).

• Take Woody's advice and make a list of some things that "need fixin'"; then make a song, poem, rap, drawing, poster, etc. about the most important ideas on the list.

Leadbelly

The King of the 12-string Guitar

LEARNING OBJECTIVES

After reading UNIT THREE and doing the activities you will be able to:

- Describe how Leadbelly's music reflects or differs from the experience of African Americans living in the United States from 1900 until 1950.
- List contributions Huddie Ledbetter made to American music.
- Identify other musicians associated with and influenced by him.
- Describe Leadbelly's musical style and his musical roots in field hollers, dance tunes, spirituals, blues, prison songs and ballads.
- Sing and/or play some of Leadbelly's songs.

LEADBELLY'S SONGS

UNIT THREE explores the life and music of Huddie Ledbetter, better known as Leadbelly. Leadbelly was one of the last of the country blues guitar players who brought us both a glimpse of the past and a look into the future where African-American music would have a dominant influence on the rise of rock 'n' roll and other musical styles. Through his recordings at the Library of Congress and Folkways Records, Leadbelly enriched our knowledge of African-American music and culture.

The life of Leadbelly is a story of both triumph and tragedy. The tragedy is that he, like other members of his race, was subjected to discrimination, economic hardship and violence. The triumph is that he was able to overcome many of these conditions and become one of the most significant figures in 20th century American folk and popular music.

LADY: *What's the matter with your guitar? What's all this writing on it?*

VAL: *Autographs of famous musicians. See this name here. Leadbelly?*

LADY: *Leadbelly?*

VAL: *Greatest man ever lived on the twelve-string guitar! Played it so good he broke the stone heart of a Texas Governor and won himself a pardon out of jail.*

—*Tennessee Williams*
from the play **Orpheus Descending**

Leadbelly's Life

Down in Louisiana

Huddie Ledbetter was born in 1885 in Mooringsport, Louisiana, in the bayous of the Mississippi Delta close to the Texas border. His father Wes was a hardworking sharecropper who taught him to plow and pick cotton. **"Cotton Fields"** (p. 32) and **"Bring Me L'il' Water, Silvy"** (p. 47) are musical sketches from his early life working in the fields as the son of a cotton farmer. His mother Sally was half African American and half Cherokee. Huddie's uncle Terrell, a major influence on his musical life, taught him to play first the "windjammer" Cajun accordion, then the guitar, mandolin, harmonica (mouth harp) and piano.

By age fifteen he had become a well known local musician who played at **sookey-jumps** (Saturday night country dance parties) and **breakdowns** (dances). During this period he visited Fannin Street, the entertainment district of Shreveport, and it was there that he heard many new kinds of music such as **barrel-house piano** (a form of early blues). Leadbelly was a favorite with the ladies and was known for his quick temper. Throughout his life, he worked hard, played hard, and his quick temper often got him into trouble with the law. In 1905 he left Louisiana and was "banished away and went out in West Texas, pickin' cotton."

In Texas, Leadbelly met **Blind Lemon Jefferson**, one of the great country blues guitarists and singers. Eventually Jefferson and Leadbelly worked as a musical team and played in Dallas and the surrounding countryside. Leadbelly learned many songs from Lemon Jefferson and used this collaboration to hone his guitar techniques to a fine edge. In Dallas, Leadbelly was introduced to the **12-string guitar** (a common instrument with Mexican folk musicians of the area, but not common among blues players). He also developed the technique of playing **slide guitar** (sometimes known as **bottleneck guitar**) with a knife blade.

In 1917, Leadbelly killed a man in a fight over a woman and was sentenced to a Texas prison farm. Life working on a prison chain gang was unbearably hard, and treatment of African-American prisoners was often cruel and inhuman. Since Leadbelly had lived a life of hard work and was an exceptionally strong man, he vowed to meet the prison challenge head-on and become a survivor. Because of his superior strength, he rose to the position of lead man on many of the chain gangs. The song **"Take This Hammer"** (p. 43) is a good example of a prison work song. The word "(wah)" inserted in this song indicates the point where the axe or hammer was struck while singing the song. In the evenings Leadbelly sang his songs for other prisoners. The song **"The Midnight Special"** (p. 41) was composed while Leadbelly was working in the Sugar Land prison farm.

The Texas prison worksong repertory had a big influence on blues singers such as Leadbelly and Blind Lemon Jefferson. Songs such as "Ain't No More Cane on the Brazos," "Roberta," "Long Hot Summer Days," "Shorty George" and "Make a Longtime Man Feel Bad" became an important part of Leadbelly's songbag. Some of the blues protest songs helped African Americans find a voice to express their anger over racial prejudice and discrimination.

Leadbelly's talent caught the ear of the prison warden and others working at the prison, and he was asked to play for special occasions. When he heard that the new Texas Governor Pat Neff and his wife were coming to the prison for a visit, he wrote a special song asking the governor to pardon him.

Nineteen hundred and twenty-three,
The judge took my liberty away from me,
Left my wife wringin' her hand and cryin',
"Lord have mercy on this man of mine."

I am your servant compose this song,
Please Governor Neff, lemme go back home,
I know my wife will jump and shout,
Train rolls up, I come stepping out.

Please, Honorable Governor, be good an' kind,
If I don't get a pardon will you cut my time?
Had you, Governor Neff, like you got me,
Wake up in the morning and I'd set you free.

The song touched the heart of the governor, who was trying to correct some of the Texas prison problems, and he pardoned Leadbelly in 1925. After release from prison, Leadbelly returned to his home in Louisiana.

Living at home in Louisiana did not bring Huddie Ledbetter peace, and within five years he was involved in a fight defending himself from an attack and was again sentenced to prison. Three years later in 1933, John Lomax, a folksong collector from the Library of Congress, visited the Angola Prison Farm where Leadbelly was located. Lomax and his son Alan were recording African-American prison work songs. The Lomaxes found Leadbelly to be an incredible source of song material from work songs to blues, dance songs, children's songs and ballads. John Lomax took a special interest in Leadbelly's case and helped get him a parole when he hand delivered another original Leadbelly song plea to Louisiana Governor Allen.

Off to New York

I was born and raised i' the country, mamma,
but I'm stayin' in town . . . in New York City,
what I'm talkin' 'bout.

The Lomaxes convinced Leadbelly to travel with them to other prisons throughout the South for the purpose of recording for the Library of Congress. Shortly thereafter Leadbelly married Martha Promise and went with the Lomaxes to Washington, D. C. and then to New York City. The song **"The Bourgeois Blues"**

(p. 31) describes Leadbelly's feelings about the housing discrimination to which he and Martha were subjected on their travels.

During his stay in New York from 1935 to 1949, Leadbelly made recordings for Columbia, Capitol, Victor, Asch, Musicraft, Disc and the Library of Congress. He sang on radio programs such as *Folk Songs of America* (WNYC) and *Back Where I Come From* (CBS Radio Network). Leadbelly toured extensively throughout the Northeast and sang concerts of his music at colleges and universities. He was much in demand in New York City for appearances at local parties, lofts, clubs and political rallies. He was a favorite with the liberals and often appeared at folk gatherings with singers such as Paul Robeson, Josh White, Sonny Terry, Brownie McGhee, Woody Guthrie (they called themselves the "Headline Singers"), Burl Ives and the Almanac Singers.

Despite Leadbelly's talent and fine recordings, he was somewhat out of step with the times. During the late 1930s and '40s other blues guitarists such as Muddy Waters were moving into a style that would be called **rhythm and blues (R&B)** or **urban blues**. This emerging style was built around a small band concept which featured electric guitar with other instruments such as saxophones, piano, bass and drums. In addition to the instrumentation, the subject matter of the songs was much more concerned with urban living than the rural life described in many of Leadbelly's songs. As a result of this shift in public tastes, Leadbelly often found himself having to work at menial jobs in order to earn a living. During these years he was kept on a recording retainer by Moe Asch of Folkways Records, and in 1948 he recorded his historic *Leadbelly's Last Sessions* (FW241). At sixty-four, Huddie Ledbetter died of "Lou Gehrig's disease" in a New York hospital.

Six months after his death, his song **"Goodnight Irene"** (p. 36) became a popular hit in a version sung by the Weavers, and the record sold over two million copies. The royalties eventually started coming in, and they eased his wife Martha's financial burden. The Weavers, including Leadbelly's friend Pete Seeger, helped to popularize Leadbelly's music and eventually his songs were sung, published and recorded by many different musicians around the world.

Leadbelly's Music

Leadbelly's music reflected his growing-up years in rural Louisiana, his years of hard prison labor, and his experience with the big cities. Some of the songs that reflect his rural upbringing include "Bring Me Li'l' Water, Silvy," "Boll Weevil," "Cotton Fields," and "Gray Goose" (sung by Sweet Honey in the Rock on the *A Vision Shared* recording and Leadbelly on *Folkways: The Original Vision*).

Because Leadbelly played for sookey-jumps, many of his songs have a distinct dance beat often including a strong bass line resembling a **boogie-woogie** pattern. Leadbelly introduced the ballad of "John Henry," the steel-drivin' man, in the following way:

Now this is "John Henry" and it's a dance tune
and we dance it down home and
I'm gonna play it for you.

Leadbelly pioneered a powerful bass-melody, 12-string guitar style that became the African-American counterpart to the bass-melody style of guitar pioneered by Maybelle Carter of the Carter Family and later picked up by Woody Guthrie. Other dance tunes played and sung by Leadbelly include "Corn Bread Rough" and "Salty Dog."

Most African-American singers and songwriters including Leadbelly have been influenced in some way by the church, spiritual or gospel traditions. Introducing the song "Look Away to Heaven" Leadbelly said:

At home when I go to the Baptist church,
the sisters in the amen corner,
they always lead out.

It is not uncommon for a blues or secular singer to also be involved in the world of gospel music. Two outstanding examples would be **Thomas Dorsey**—"the father of African American gospel"—who was an outstanding blues composer and pianist, and **Aretha Franklin**—"soul sister number one"—who is at home with rock or "Amazing Grace." Other Leadbelly songs that reflect this gospel tradition include "We Shall Walk Through the Valley" and "They Hung Him On a Cross."

Leadbelly's prison experiences yielded some of his most powerful songs. In addition to "The Midnight Special" and "Take This Hammer," there is "Black Betty," "Didn't Old John" (a work song influenced by the spiritual tradition), "Go Down Old Hannah," "Julie Ann Johnson" and "On a Monday."

The blues songs including "Good Morning Blues," "The Bourgeois Blues" (p. 31), "Jailhouse Blues" and "Leavin' Blues" are some of Leadbelly's best material. Leadbelly said:

. . . when you lay down at night, turn from one side of the bed all night to the other and you can't sleep, what's the matter? Blues got you. Or when you get up in the mornin', sit on side of the bed—may have a mother or father, sister or brother, boy friend or girl friend, husband or a wife around—you don't want no talk out of um. They ain't done you nothin', you ain't done them nothin'—what's the matter? Blues got you.

Leadbelly, like Woody Guthrie, loved playing and singing for children. Some of his children's songs include "Red Bird," "Ha Ha This A-Way" and a cowboy song from his horse-breaking days in Texas called "Cow Cow Yicky Yicky Yea."

In the book *The Leadbelly Songbook*, Frederic Ramsey Jr. describes Leadbelly's singing in the following way:

Leadbelly's voice was not beautiful. It was rough and grainy, and some of its raw tones came up as if scraped out of his throat. It rang out with intensity because he often shouted with violence. It had a nasal twang. The excitement he engendered came from his understanding of each melody he sang and from a strong, precise sense of rhythm. He played his own twelve-string guitar, and its tempo fell in with each type of song; for breakdowns, the strings zinged at breakneck time; but he held the slow blues to an even, carefully marked beat, usually in low register. Leadbelly was set apart from other folk singers by his extraordinary ability to tell a story, and a repertoire that included blues, work songs, slave songs, shouts, hollers, reels, railroad and prison songs, ballads, spirituals, cowboy, popular, and play songs. And above all, he was not afraid—not afraid to run up and down a scale that took in baritone and tenor registers along the way, but didn't stick to either. The hollers he yelled out were almost impossible of notation in our Occidental music scale. He was not afraid to shift pitch, and he often accelerated tempo to suit mood and action.

Leadbelly's Influence

Leadbelly's influence started in New York. His associations with Woody Guthrie, Sonny Terry, Cisco Houston, Brownie McGhee, Paul Robeson, Burl Ives, the Almanac Singers, Oscar Brand, and others helped lay the foundations for the Folk Revival of the 1950s. On the *Folkways: The Original Vision* recording, Leadbelly collaborates with Guthrie, Houston and Terry on the song, "We Shall Be Free." Woody Guthrie was impressed by Leadbelly's ready sense of rhyme and his ability to sing for any crowd:

> I've heard him say to a padded roomful of upper class folks, "You folks are mine, I'll sing for you fine." And heard him yell out above the wild smokey clatter of an odd colored, loose nail, rattle board room packed with the freest of prancing dancers, " You folks are my best, I'll sing your request." I've seen him laugh and joke with school kids, nursery kids, little toddlers climbing all over his guitar and up and down his arms and legs, and tell them, "You make me feel new, I'll sing best for you."

Pete Seeger became a champion of Leadbelly's music and guitar styling. He published *The 12-String Guitar as Played by Leadbelly*, and with the Weavers, popularized many of Leadbelly's songs during the 1950s and '60s. Seeger comments on Leadbelly's influence on him—

> Looking back, I think that the most important thing I learned from him was the straightforward approach, the direct honesty. He bequeathed to us also, it is true, a couple hundred of the best songs any of us will ever know.

The Liverpool pop singer Lonnie Donnegan reworked many of Leadbelly's songs to create the skiffle band sound, and many of the '60s English rock groups such as the Beatles grew up playing them.

Alan Lomax, folklorist, author and friend, had this to say about him:

> Leadbelly left his mark on his era; his steel voice, his steel arm on the twelve strings and his high-voltage personality captured audiences everywhere. More than any other singer, he demonstrated to a streamlined, city-oriented world that America had living folk music— swamp primitive, angry, freighted with great sorrow and great joy.

Unit Review

REVIEW QUESTIONS

1. How do the songs "Bring Me Li'l' Water, Silvy," "Cotton Fields," "Take This Hammer" and "The Midnight Special" reflect Leadbelly's life in Louisiana and Texas?

2. Who influenced Leadbelly's musical style? What instruments did he play?

3. How does the song "The Bourgeois Blues" deal with racial discrimination? Can you find other songs about this subject?

4. Who were some of the musicians influenced by Leadbelly?

5. What are the differences you hear and see between the songs of Leadbelly and those of Woody Guthrie?

MORE ABOUT LEADBELLY

If you would like to read more about Leadbelly and hear more of his music, try these:

Asch, Moses and Alan Lomax, eds. *The Leadbelly Songbook.* New York: Oak, 1962.

Leadbelly. New York: Trio Folkways Music, 1976. —a songbook

Lomax, John A. and Alan. *Negro Folksongs as Sung by Lead Belly.* New York: MacMillan, 1936.

Leadbelly's Last Sessions. (Folkways Records 2941 A/B, C/D; 2942 A/B, C/D).

Recordings —see listing of other Leadbelly recordings on liner notes to *Folkways: The Original Vision.* Smithsonian Folkways.

CREATIVE PROJECTS

• Try making up a12-bar blues in the style of "The Bourgeois Blues" (p. 31). Remember Leadbelly's description of the blues on page 22, and sing about whatever's got you down.

• Make up new 2-line verses for "Rock Island Line" (p. 42), keeping in mind that they can be borrowed from most African-American spirituals (See page 6 for more information.)

The New Generation

Musicians featured on the video tape and recording

A Vision Shared: A Tribute to Woody Guthrie and Leadbelly

The new generation of artists featured on the *A Vision Shared* video tape and recording have taken the songs of Woody Guthrie and Leadbelly and transformed them into contemporary versions flavored by the influences of rock, blues, and country music. In some cases, the use of electrified instruments gives the music a hard edge that really drives home the original meaning of the song. The comments of the artists on the video tape show the continuity of both style and intention that binds the new generation to the old.

Bob Dylan

Bob Dylan [Robert Allen Zimmerman] was born May 24, 1941 in Duluth, Minnesota. During his early days in Hibbing, Minnesota, Dylan taught himself to play guitar, harmonica, and piano. In 1959 he attended the University of Minnesota where he fell in love with folk music, and in 1961 he travelled to New York to visit his idol, Woody Guthrie. It was in the coffeehouses of New York's Greenwich Village that Dylan first made his mark. His 1963 album *The Freewheelin' Bob Dylan* revealed him to be the songwriter and poet for the times with such hits as "A Hard Rain's A-Gonna Fall," "Masters of War," and the superhit, "Blowin' in the Wind." His 1964 song, "The Times They Are A-Changin'," foreshadowed a decade of social change. In 1965, his electric guitar performance at the Newport Folk Festival and the Byrds' recording of his "Mr. Tambourine Man" ushered in the **folk-rock** movement. Later hit songs include "Like a Rolling Stone," "All Along the Watchtower," and "Lay Lady Lay." Dylan has experimented with many styles including rock, country, and gospel. His songs and lyrics have influenced performers such as Bruce Springsteen, Elvis Costello, Rod Stewart, and Tom Petty. His songs have been performed by nearly everyone from Joan Baez to Eric Clapton and Stevie Wonder.

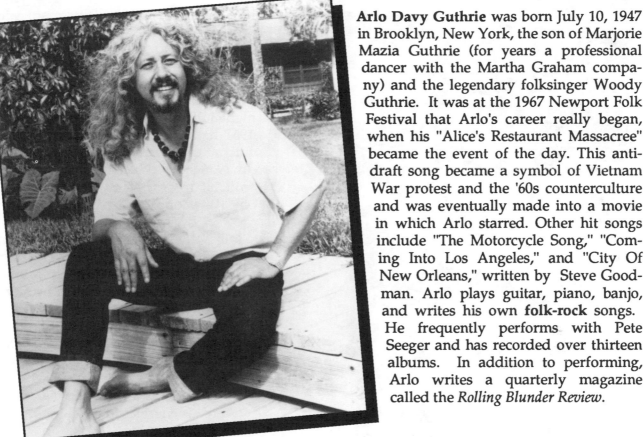

Arlo Guthrie

Arlo Davy Guthrie was born July 10, 1947 in Brooklyn, New York, the son of Marjorie Mazia Guthrie (for years a professional dancer with the Martha Graham company) and the legendary folksinger Woody Guthrie. It was at the 1967 Newport Folk Festival that Arlo's career really began, when his "Alice's Restaurant Massacree" became the event of the day. This anti-draft song became a symbol of Vietnam War protest and the '60s counterculture and was eventually made into a movie in which Arlo starred. Other hit songs include "The Motorcycle Song," "Coming Into Los Angeles," and "City Of New Orleans," written by Steve Goodman. Arlo plays guitar, piano, banjo, and writes his own **folk-rock** songs. He frequently performs with Pete Seeger and has recorded over thirteen albums. In addition to performing, Arlo writes a quarterly magazine called the *Rolling Blunder Review*.

Emmylou Harris was born April 12, 1947 in Birmingham, Alabama. Although she was exposed to country music as she grew up, Emmylou began her career as an urban folksinger and guitar player in New York's Greenwich Village. After her brief stint in New York City, she moved to Washington, D.C., where she worked with the legendary Gram Parsons until his death in 1973. In 1975 she recorded her first breakthrough **country** hit with "If I Could Only Win Your Love." Other hits include "Sweet Dreams," "One of These Days," "Make Believe," "Mister Sandman," "Blue Kentucky Girl," and "To Daddy." Emmylou Harris has performed and recorded with top stars such as Dolly Parton, Linda Ronstadt, Buck Owens, Don Williams, Ricky Scaggs, and Roy Orbison. She has received numerous awards including the Grammy and many Country Music Awards.

Emmylou Harris

Little Richard [Richard Penniman] was born on December 25, 1935 in Macon, Georgia. Richard grew up playing piano and singing in the church choir. He got his first professional experience as a **rhythm and blues** musician in a Macon nightclub run by his foster parents. In 1951 he signed his first recording contract after entering a contest in Atlanta. In 1956 he produced his first **rock 'n' roll** hit record, "Tutti Frutti," (covered by Pat Boone), which was quickly followed by six more including "Long Tall Sally," "Keep a Knockin'," and "Good Golly, Miss Molly." On stage, Little Richard created an explosion of energy that was unmatched by any of his contemporaries in the first generation of rock 'n' roll. He influenced many other performers such as James Brown, Otis Redding, and the Beatles. Twice Little Richard has given up his life as a rock musician to devote his energies to the church.

Little Richard

Taj Mahal [Henry Sainte Claire Fredricks], born on May 17, 1940 in New York, is the son of a West Indian jazz musician father and a South Carolina gospel singer mother. Taj is a self-taught master of many instruments including finger-style guitar, banjo, piano, harmonica, mandolin, bass, vibes, and kalimba. He emerged professionally in 1965 as a co-founder (with guitarist Ry Cooder) of The Rising Sons, and he went on to establish a career as one of the foremost interpreters of African-American roots music including **blues, jazz, West African, and Caribbean** styles. In addition to numerous recordings and concert tours, Taj Mahal has acted in films (*Sounder I* and *II*) and television productions.

Taj Mahal

John Cougar Mellencamp

John Cougar Mellencamp was born October 7, 1951 in Seymour, Indiana. After high school he got married and moved to Louisville, Kentucky. He worked as a guitarist, singer, and songwriter in Midwestern rock bands before finally getting his first recording break in 1975. During the '70s, John recorded a number of moderately successful records, and his straightforward mainstream **rock** style was often compared to Bob Seger or Bruce Springsteen. In 1982 *American Fool* catapulted to the top of the charts to become his first platinum record with the hit singles "Hurts So Good" and "Jack & Diane." By 1984 Billboard had ranked him in its top 10 Pop Album Artists—Male. Other albums include *Uh-Huh* with singles "Pink Houses" and "Crumblin' Down"; *Scarecrow* with singles "Small Town," "Lonely Ol' Night," and "R.O.C.K. in the U.S.A."; *The Lonesome Jubilee*, and *Big Daddy*. Along the way John Cougar Mellencamp has taken time out of his busy touring schedule to contribute his talent to such causes as the Farm Aid concerts.

Willie Nelson was born on April 30, 1933 in Abbott, Texas. At age six, Willie was given a Stella guitar by his father, and he grew up influenced by gospel music, country-western music from the Grand Ole Opry, jazz, blues, Mexican music, and Bob Wills' brand of Texas western swing. He worked for many years as a relatively unknown **country** singer and guitar player in Texas, and in 1960 he moved to Nashville where he served as a songwriter for stars such as Patsy Cline and Ray Price. In 1970 he left Nashville to return to Austin, Texas, where he became the leader of "the outlaws"—a group of musicians, including Waylon Jennings, who rebelled against the Nashville country music establishment. His 1973 record, *Shotgun Willie*, was the first of many that have made him a superstar of country music. His more than thirty albums include the hit songs "Blue Eyes Crying in the Rain," "Georgia On My Mind," "Mamas Don't Let Your Babies Grow Up to Be Cowboys," "On the Road Again," "Always On My Mind," and "Good Hearted Woman."

Willie Nelson

Pete Seeger

Pete Seeger, born on May 3, 1919 in Patterson, New York, is the son of musicologist Charles Seeger and violinist Constance Edson Seeger. It wasn't long before Pete picked up the five-string banjo and guitar. After dropping out of Harvard, he assisted Alan Lomax at the Library of Congress and then returned to New York City to form the Almanac Singers. Later Seeger and Woody Guthrie toured the country singing for union halls and migrant worker camps. After World War II, he started People's Songs, Inc., the forerunner of *Sing Out!* magazine. In 1949 Seeger, Lee Hays, Ronnie Gilbert, and Fred Hellerman formed a new **folk** group called the Weavers, which sold more than four million records and started the Folk Music Revival. Although he was blacklisted during the '50s McCarthy era, Seeger continued to work for causes such as civil rights, the cleanup of the Hudson River, world peace, and jobs for all. His hit songs include "Where Have All the Flowers Gone?," "If I Had a Hammer," and "Turn, Turn, Turn."

Bruce Springsteen was born on September 23, 1949 in Freehold, New Jersey. At age 13 he learned to play guitar and joined a rock band called the Castiles, for which he wrote songs during his high school years. In 1972, John Hammond of CBS records discovered him, and Springsteen assembled the E Street Band to make his first successful recording *Greetings from Asbury Park, N.J.* By 1975, Springsteen had released his *Born to Run* album to a flurry of publicity including cover stories on *Time* and *Newsweek* magazines. In 1984, his album *Born in the U.S.A.* firmly established him as "The Boss" of mainstream **rock**. It featured the hit singles "Born in the U.S.A.," "Dancing in the Dark," and "Cover Me." Springsteen played a key role in the *We Are the World* video and album, which was produced to aid world hunger. The five-record *Live* set from 1988 culminated a decade of work with the E Street Band. His *Tunnel of Love* album marked not only a new direction, but his status as the only artist during the 1980s to score four number one LPs in *Billboard*.

Bruce Springsteen

Sweet Honey in The Rock

Sweet Honey in The Rock is a quintet of African-American women from Washington, D.C. who sing **unaccompanied** except for body and hand percussion instruments. This unique vocal group was founded in 1973 under the leadership of Bernice Johnson Reagon, vocal director of the D.C. Black Repertory Theatre. The strength of Sweet Honey in The Rock lies within their sound and repertoire, which is rooted in the tradition of the African-American unaccompanied congregational style and embraces its many extensions. You can hear the moan of the blues, the power of early twentieth century gospel, echoes of the community a cappella quartet, jazz choral vocalizations, the sound of African singing, and much more. Current members of the group (clockwise from the left) are Bernice Johnson Reagon, Aisha Kahlil, Shirley Childress Johnson (sign language interpreter), Evelyn Maria Harris, Ysaye Maria Barnwell and Nitanju Bolade.

U2 is a rock vocal and instrumental group from Ireland consisting of Paul "Bono" Hewson (b. 1960), Dave "The Edge" Evans (b. 1961), Adam Clayton (b. 1960), and Larry Mullen (b. 1962). The band was formed in Dublin during the late '70s when the punk movement was in fashion, but right from the start they decided to play straight-ahead **rock** unlike the "bands in satin trousers who take the money and run." In the early days the band played under a tin-roofed parking lot to teenagers who came to hear them, but by 1979 they had been discovered by CBS and signed to Island Records. By 1983 U2 had become an international supergroup with the platinum album *War*. In 1987, the album *The Joshua Tree* became Grammy Album of the Year with the singles "With or Without You" and "I Still Haven't Found What I'm Looking For." The 1988 album *Rattle and Hum* was also made into a film.

U2

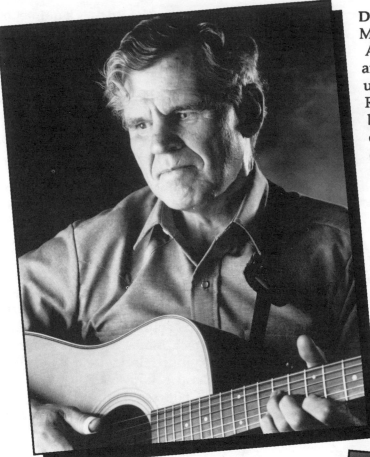

Doc Watson [Arthel Lane] was born on March 2, 1923 in Deep Gap, North Carolina. A **country** music singer, harmonica, guitar, and banjo player, Watson played locally until he was discovered by folklorist Ralph Rinzler in 1960. Despite the handicap of blindness, Doc Watson went on to become one of the greatest guitar players alive today. His breakthrough public appearance came in 1963 when he sang and played at the Newport Folk Festival. In 1971 he joined "Mother" Maybelle Carter, Earl Scruggs, Roy Acuff, Merle Travis, and the Nitty Gritty Dirt Band on the classic album *Will the Circle Be Unbroken.* Watson often performed in a duo with his son Merle until Merle's untimely death in an accident in the late '80s. Doc Watson is best known for his flat-picking guitar style, which has influenced a whole generation of younger **bluegrass** players such as Tony Rice, Clarence White, Norman Blake, and Dan Crary.

Doc Watson

Brian Wilson was born on June 20, 1942 in Hawthorne, California. Brian Wilson, along with Alan Jardine, Mike Love, Dennis Wilson, and Carl Wilson, formed the **Beach Boys**, who are credited with creating the '60s surf music craze. The group began as a local **rock** band in 1961 and reached national attention in 1963 with a tour and their first album *Surfin' U.S.A.* Some of the Beach Boys' greatest hits written by Brian Wilson include "Good Vibrations," "Surfin' U.S.A.," "California Girls," "Barbara Ann," and "I Get Around." The group reached its highest popularity during the period from 1963 to '66, after which Brian Wilson stopped touring with the group. By the late '70s, the members of the band were pursuing their own recording projects, but in 1981 they came back together for a twentieth anniversary concert. In 1983 Brian Wilson rejoined the group tours, and the Beach Boys were invited to perform at President Reagan's inaugural ball. Shortly thereafter, Wilson embarked on a solo career with an album entitled *Brian Wilson.*

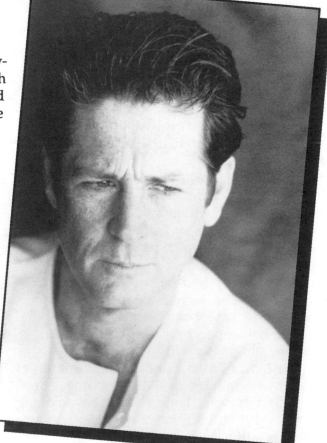

Brian Wilson

The Songs

Please, please, please, don't read nor sing my songs like no lesson book, like no text for today.
But let them be a little key to sort of unlock and let down all your old bars.

—Woody Guthrie

The music which follows represents the songs as sung by Woody Guthrie and Leadbelly rather than the newer versions found on the *A Vision Shared* video tape and recording. The songs are pitched in easy-to-sing keys with chord symbols for instruments such as guitars and Autoharps. Make the songs your own—transpose them, make your own versions, and add new verses.

The Bourgeois Blues

Words and Music by Huddie Ledbetter
Edited with new additional material
by Alan Lomax

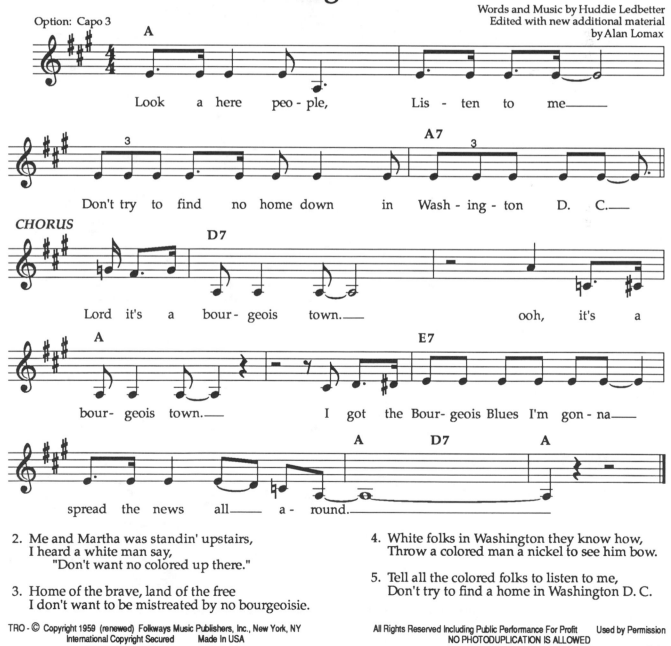

2. Me and Martha was standin' upstairs,
   I heard a white man say,
      "Don't want no colored up there."

3. Home of the brave, land of the free
   I don't want to be mistreated by no bourgeoisie.

4. White folks in Washington they know how,
   Throw a colored man a nickel to see him bow.

5. Tell all the colored folks to listen to me,
   Don't try to find a home in Washington D.C.

Cotton Fields
(The Cotton Song)

Words and Music by
Huddie Ledbetter

When I was a lit-tle ba-by my moth-er would
It may sound a lit-tle fun-ny, But you did-n't
I was o-ver in Ar-kan-sas, Peo-ple ask me,

rock me in the cra-dle in them old, old cot-ton fields at
make ve-ry much mon-ey In them old___ cot-ton fields at
What you come here for In them old___ cot-ton fields at

home.___ When I was a lit-tle ba-by my moth-er would
home.___ It may sound a lit-tle fun-ny, But you did-n't
home.___ I was o-ver in Ar-kan-sas, Peo-ple ask me,

rock me in the cra-dle in them old___ cot-ton fields at home.___
make ve-ry much mon-ey in them old___ cot-ton fields at home.___
What you come here for In them old___ cot-ton fields at home.___

CHORUS

Oh, when them cot-ton balls get rot-ten you could-n't pick ve-ry much cot-ton, in them

old cot-ton fields at home. It was down in Lou'-si-an-a, Just a

mile from Tex-ar-ka-na, in them old___ cot-ton fields at home.

Deportee
(Plane Wreck at Los Gatos)

Lyric by Woody Guthrie
Music by Martin Hoffman

Selected verses

The crops are all in and the peach-es are
My fa-ther's own fa-ther, he wad-ed that
Some of us are il-le-gal and some are not

rot-t'ning, The or-ang-es piled in their cre-o-sote
riv-er, They took all the mon-ey he made in his
want-ed, Our work contract's out and we have to move

dumps; You're fly-ing 'em back to the Mex-i-can
life; My broth-ers and sis-ters come work-ing the
on; Six hun-dred miles to that Mex-i-can

bor-der, To pay all their mon-ey to wade back a-gain.
fruit trees, And they rode the truck till they took down and died.
bor-der, They chase us like out-laws, like rus-tlers, like thieves.

CHORUS

Good-bye to my Juan, good-bye, Ro-sa-li-ta, A-

dios, mis a-mi-gos, Je-sus y Ma-ri-a; You

won't have your names when you ride the big air-plane,

All they will call you will be de-por-tees.

33

Do Re Mi

Words and Music by
Woody Guthrie

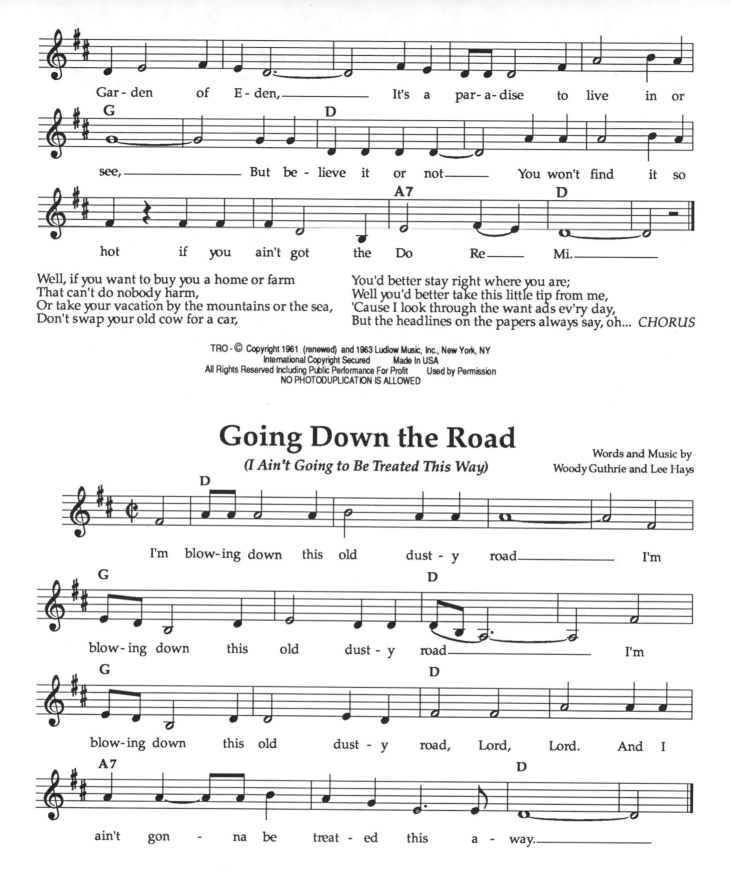

Gar-den of E-den, It's a par-a-dise to live in or

G ... **D**

see, But be-lieve it or not You won't find it so

A7 ... **D**

hot if you ain't got the Do Re Mi.

Well, if you want to buy you a home or farm
That can't do nobody harm,
Or take your vacation by the mountains or the sea,
Don't swap your old cow for a car,

You'd better stay right where you are;
Well you'd better take this little tip from me,
'Cause I look through the want ads ev'ry day,
But the headlines on the papers always say, oh... *CHORUS*

Going Down the Road
(I Ain't Going to Be Treated This Way)

Words and Music by
Woody Guthrie and Lee Hays

D

I'm blow-ing down this old dust-y road I'm

G ... **D**

blow-ing down this old dust-y road I'm

G ... **D**

blow-ing down this old dust-y road, Lord, Lord. And I

A7 ... **D**

ain't gon - na be treat-ed this a-way.

2. I'm going where the water tastes like wine, (3x)
   And I ain't gonna be treated this away.

3. I'm going where them dust storms never blow, (3x)
   And I ain't gonna be treated this away.

4. They say I'm a dust bowl refugee, (3x)
   And I ain't gonna be treated this away.

5. I'm looking for a job with honest pay, (3x)
   And I ain't gonna be treated this away.

Goodnight Irene

Words and Music by
Huddie Ledbetter and John A. Lomax

CHORUS

I - rene good night_____ I - rene good night_____ Good night, I - rene, Good night I - rene, I'll kiss you in my dreams._____

VERSE

Some - times I live in the coun - try_____ Some - times I live_____ in town._____ Some - times I have a great no - tion_____ to jump in - to the ri - ver and drown._____

I asked your mo - ther for you,_____ She told me you were too young._____ I wish to the Lord I never seen your face, I'm sor - ry you ev - er was born._____

You caused me to weep, you caused me to moan, You caused me to leave my home._____ The last word I ev - er heard her say, "I want you to sing me a song."_____

Stop ram - bling and_____ stop gam - bling,_____ Quit stay - ing out late at night._____ Go home to your wife and your family,_____ Sit down by the fire - side bright._____

Fine

D.C. al Fine

Hard Travelin'

Words and Music by
Woody Guthrie

4. I've been working that Pittsburgh steel, I thought you knowed,
   I've been pouring redhot slag, way down the road,
   I've been blasting, I've been firing, I've been pouring redhot iron,
   And I've been having some hard traveling, Lord.

5. I been laying in a hardrock jail, I thought you knowed,
   I been laying out ninety days, way down that road,
   Mean old judge he says to me, It's ninety days for vagrancy,
   And I've been hitting some hard traveling, Lord.

Hobo's Lullaby
(Woody's Favorite)

Words and Music by
Goebel Reeves

I Ain't Got No Home

Words and Music by
Woody Guthrie

I've Got to Know

Words and Music by
Woody Guthrie

CHORUS

I've got to know,— yes, I've got to know, friend; Hun-gry lips ask me wher-ev-er I go!— Com-rades and friends all— a-fall-ing a-round me, I've got to know, yes, I've got to know!

VERSE

Why do your war boats ride on my wa-ters?— Why do your
What makes your boats haul death to my peo-ple?— Ni-tro block-
Why can't my two hands get a good pay job?— I can still

death bombs fall from my skies?— Tell me, why do you
bus-ters, big cannons and guns? — Why don't your
plow and plant, I can still sow!— Why did your law-

burn my farm and my town down? I've— got to
ships bring food and some cloth-ing? I've sure got to
book chase me off my good land? I'd sure like to

know, friend, I've— got to know!
know, folks, I've sure got to know!
know, friend, I've just got to know!

4. What good work did you do, I'd like to ask you,
To give you my money right out of my hands?
I built your big house here to hide from my people;
Why do you crave to hide so, I'd love to know!

5. You keep me in jail and you lock me in prison;
Your hospital's jammed and your crazyhouse full;
What made your cop kill my trade union worker?
You have to talk plain, 'cause I sure have to know!

6. Why can't I get work and cash a big paycheck?
Why can't I buy things in your place and your store?
Why close my plant down and starve all my buddies?
I'm asking you sir, 'cause I've sure got to know!

The Midnight Special

Words and Music by Huddie Ledbetter
Collected and adapted by
John A. Lomax and Alan Lomax

Rock Island Line

Words and Music by Huddie Ledbetter
Edited with new additional material
by Alan Lomax

Selected verses

CHORUS

Oh the Rock Is-Land Line— is a might-y good road— Oh— the

Rock Is-land Line— is the road to ride— Oh— the

Rock Is-land Line— is a might-y good road— If— you

want to ride it got to ride it like you find it get your

tick-et at the sta-tion at the Rock Is-land Line.—

VERSE

A B C dou-ble X Y Z

I may be right and I may be wrong

Cats in the cup-board, but they don't— see me.—
You gon-na miss me— when— I'm gone.—

Take This Hammer

Words and music adapted and arranged
by John A. Lomax and Alan Lomax

3. If he asks you... was I laughin' ... (3x)
   Tell him I was cryin'... tell him I was cryin'.

4. I don't want no... cold iron shackles... (3x)
   Around my leg... around my leg.

5. I don't want no corn bread, peas and molasses...(3x)
   Hurts my pride...hurts my pride.

This Land Is Your Land

Words and Music by
Woody Guthrie

4. When the sun came shining, and I was strolling,
And the wheat fields waving and the dust clouds rolling,
As the fog was lifting a voice was chanting:
This land was made for you and me.

5. As I went walking, I saw a sign there,
And on the sign it said "No Trespassing."
But on the other side it didn't say nothing,
That side was made for you and me.

6. In the shadows of the steepl I saw my people,
By the Relief Office I seen my people;
As they stood there hungry, I stood there asking
Is this land was made for you and me?

7. Nobody living can ever stop me,
As I go walking that freedom highway;
Nobody living can ever make me turn back,
This land was made for you and me.

Union Maid

Words and Music by
Woody Guthrie

Vigilante Man

Words and Music by
Woody Guthrie

Option: Capo 2 or 3

Have you seen____ that vig - i - lan - te man?____
Well, what is____ a vig - i - lan - te man?____
Rain - y night____ down in the en - gine house,____

— Have you seen that vig - i - lan - te man?____
— Tell me what is a vig - i - lan - te man?____
— Sleep - ing just as still as a mouse.____

— Have____ you seen that vig - i - lan - te
— Has____ he got a club____ in his
— Man come a - long____ and chased us out____ in the

man? I've been hear - ing his name all o - ver the land.____
hand? Is that____ a vig - i - lan - te man?____
rain, Was that____ a vig - i - lan - te man?____

4. Stormy days we'd pass the time away
   Sleeping in some good warm place
   A cop come along and we give him a little race,
   Say, was that a vigilante man?

5. Preacher Casey was just a working man,
   And he said, unite all us working men,
   They killed him in the river, some strange man,
   Was that your vigilante man?

6. Oh, why does a vigilante man
   Oh, why does a vigilante man
   Carry that sawed off shotgun in his hand?
   Would he shoot his brother and sister down?

7. I rambled around from town to town
   I rambled around from town to town
   And they herded us around like a wild herd of cattle
   Was that your vigilante man?

8. Repeat verse 1

Bring Me Li'l' Water, Silvy

Words and Music by Huddie Ledbetter; Collected and adapted by John A. Lomax and Alan Lomax

```
           G                                      D7  G            C              G
CHORUS: Bring me li'l' water, Silvy. Bring me li'l' water now. Bring me li'l' water, Silvy. Ev'ry li'l' once in a while.
```

1. Don't you see me comin', Don't you see me now, Don't you see me comin', Ev'ry li'l' once in a while? *CHORUS*

2. See me come a-runnin', See me comin' now, See me come a-runnin', Ev'ry li'l' once in a while. *CHORUS*

3. Bring me the bucket, Silvy, Bring me the bucket, now, Bring me the bucket, Silvy, Ev'ry li'l' once in a while. *CHORUS*

4. Silvy come a-runnin', Silvy comin' now, Silvy come a-runnin', Ev'ry li'l' once in a while. *CHORUS*

Ramblin' 'Round

Words by Woody Guthrie; Music based on "Goodnight Irene" (p. 36) by Huddie Ledbetter and John A. Lomax

```
   G                D7                   G
1. Ramblin' around your city, Ramblin' around your town.
                 C              D7          G          D7          G
   I never see a friend I know As I go ramblin' around, boys, As I go ramblin' around.   (The last musical phrase repeats.)
```

2. My sweetheart and my parents I left in my old home town.
   I'm out to do the best I can   As I go ramblin' around, boys, As I go ramblin' around.

3. The peach trees they are loaded; The limbs are bending down.
   I pick 'em all day for a dollar, boys, As I go ramblin' around, boys, As I go ramblin' around.

4. Sometimes the fruit gets rotten, Falls down on the ground.
   There's a hungry mouth for every peach As I go ramblin' around, boys, As I go ramblin' around.

5. I wish that I could marry; I wish I could settle down;
   But I can't save a penny, boys, As I go ramblin' around, boys, As I go ramblin' around.

6. My mother prayed that I would be A man of some renown;
   But I am just a refugee, boys, As I go ramblin' around, boys, As I go ramblin' around.

Roll On, Columbia

Words by Woody Guthrie; Music based on "Goodnight Irene" (p. 36) by Huddie Ledbetter and John A. Lomax

```
             G      D7              G
CHORUS:   Roll on, Columbia, roll on,   Roll on, Columbia, roll on.
                         C              D7              G
          Your power is turning our darkness to dawn, So roll on, Columbia, roll on!
```

1. Green Douglas firs where the waters cut through, Down her wild mountains and canyons she flew.
   Canadian Northwest to the ocean so blue, Roll on, Columbia, roll on!   *CHORUS.*

2. Other great rivers add power to you, Yakima, Snake and the Klickitat too,
   Sandy Willamette and Hood River too, Roll on, Columbia, roll on!   *CHORUS.*

3. Tom Jefferson's vision would not let him rest, An empire he saw in the Pacific Northwest.
   Sent Lewis and Clark and they did the rest, Roll on, Columbia, roll on!   *CHORUS.*

4. It's there on your banks that we fought many a fight, Sheridan's boys in the blockhouse that night,
   They saw us in death but never in flight, Roll on, Columbia, roll on!   *CHORUS.*

5. At Bonneville now there are ships in the locks, The waters have risen and cleared all the rocks,
   Shiploads of plenty will steam past the docks, So roll on, Columbia, roll on!   *CHORUS.*

6. And on up the river is Grand Coulee Dam, The mightiest thing ever built by a man,
   To run the great factories and water the land, It's roll on, Columbia, roll on!   *CHORUS.*

7. These mighty men labored by day and by night, Matching their strength 'gainst the river's wild flight,
   Through rapids and falls they won the hard fight, Roll on, Columbia, roll on!   *CHORUS.*

Guitar Chords

A
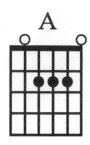

A7

Am
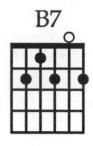

B7
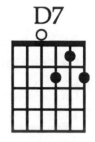

C
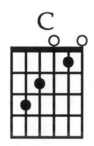

C7
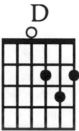

D

D7

Dm
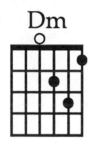

E
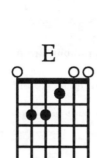

E7
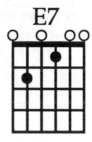

Em

G
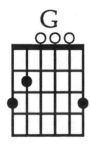

G7
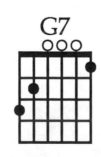

● = Depress these strings with your fingers.

O = Play these strings open.

Strings that have neither a ● nor a O should not be strummed.